The "Atocha" Treasure

THE GREAT ADVENTURES SERIES
The "Atocha" Treasure

Sara Gennings

With photographs by: Pat Clyne

Rourke Enterprises, Inc.
Vero Beach, Florida 32964

Kane Fisher, left, inspects a find of over
75 gold bars and discs.

LIBRARY OF CONGRESS
Library of Congress Cataloging-in-Publication Data

Gennings, Cara, 1954-
  The "Atocha" treasure / by Sara Gennings.

     p. cm. — (Great adventure series)
  Includes index.
  Summary: Describes the search for and the
discovery of two Spanish treasure ships lost off
the Florida Keys in a hurricane more than 300
years ago.
  ISBN 0-86592-874-6
  1.Nuestra Señora de Atocha (Ship) — Juvenile
literature. 2. Treasure-trove — Florida —Juvenile
literature. [1. Nuestra Señora de Atocha (Ship)
2. Buried treasure — Florida.] I. Title. II. Series.
G530.N82G46 1988   88-12120
917.59 - dc19   CIP
                                              AC

© 1988 Rourke Enterprises, Inc.

CONTENTS

Treasure!

It was June 1971. Under the blazing sun the treasure hunters' boats were methodically searching an area of the seabed near Key West, Florida. It was monotonous work, and for the past five years, one day had been pretty much like another. "We've got a **magnetometer** reading," called one of the crew. "Looks like a big piece of metal down there." The divers calmly pulled on their scuba gear while buoys were thrown overboard to mark the spot. They wondered what they would find this time. So far, the magnetometer readings had found nothing more than scrap metal on the seabed.

Only Mel Fisher felt any excitement as he swam down through the warm green water. Every day for five years he left the dock with his boats and crew for the open sea with the cheery words "today's the day." Perhaps, at last, today would be the day: the day he would find the treasure ships.

He emerged a few minutes later with a small, round object. It was a seventeenth-century lead musket ball. This was no scrap metal. In the same dive, his crew found a galleon anchor. Had they found one of the two lost Spanish treasure ships?

Over the next few days and weeks, more musket balls, three swords, and other artifacts were found in the area. And then — gold. An eight-and-one-half-foot-long gold chain, a gold coin minted in Spain, and two gold bars. But it was obvious that this was only a very small part of the treasure. Where was the rest?

Mel Fisher, president and founder of Treasure Salvors, Inc., displays some of the gold bars and chains.

Two gold bars glint on the seabed.

An aerial view of the Atocha wrecksite shows the blast holes made in the sand by the salvage boat's mailboxes.

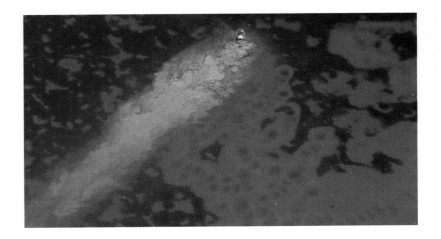

It was two years before the next major find. The treasure hunters had been patiently following the thin trickle of treasure southeast from the galleon anchor, and suddenly began to uncover hundreds of silver pieces of four and eight. So many coins were found here that the treasure hunters called the area the "Bank of Spain." Other finds included gold rings, more gold chains, and a priceless golden cup set with emeralds.

But there was no proof that any of the treasure had come from either of the two Spanish treasure ships. By now, Mel Fisher had spent seven years and a lot of money looking for the two galleons. To help financially, he had invited people to invest money in his treasure hunt, and now he had to prove to them that their money was safe. Fisher felt sure he had found one of the ships — he was not sure which — but he had to link the treasure back to one of them.

Fisher had a old friend, Dr. Eugene Lyon, who had been doing some research in the Spanish archives in Seville, Spain. It was Dr. Lyon who had realized that Fisher had at first been searching the wrong area for the galleons. He had found that an old document had been wrongly translated, giving completely wrong information as to where the galleons had sunk. Fisher moved his team to the new location advised by Dr. Lyon, and it was there that the first treasure was found.

Mel Fisher (left) and historian Dr. Eugene Lyon (right) read over some Spanish manifest documents that have been translated into English.

Dr. Lyon had also uncovered something else in the Spanish records. He had the shipping lists, or **manifests**, for the two galleons. These itemized every single thing carried by the ships at every stage of the journey. He even found a passenger list for each of the vessels.

The weaponry, jewelry, and coinage could be dated back to seventeenth-century Spain. If Fisher could match one of the finds on the seabed to one of the manifests, then he could not only prove he had found one of the galleons, but he could also tell which one it was and how much treasure there was to bring up.

A painting of Catherine, daughter of King Philip II of Spain by the artist Coello. Note the similarity of the pieces in her chain to those discovered on the Atocha site.

This model of the Atocha was made by Captain Bill Frank.

The *Atocha's* Last Voyage

In the Spanish archives, Dr. Eugene Lyon pieced together the story of the two lost Spanish galleons. The *Santa Margarita* and the *Nuestra Señora de Atocha* sailed from Spain in 1622, bound for the Spanish colonies in Central and South America. The two galleons, owned and operated by the Spanish Crown, acted as guard vessels for the merchant fleet.

In 1622, Spain had many enemies. She spent millions of pesos on her wars in Europe. Her ships were frequently attacked by the Dutch, the French, and the English. The merchant fleet needed the strong protection provided by the powerful armed galleons. For this protection, the merchants paid the Spanish Crown a twenty-percent tax on the profits of their trade with the colonies.

Before setting sail for Havana, Cuba, the 1622 fleet traded Spanish goods for Peruvian silver, and gold from the mines of Colombia. This was to be their last port of call before the homeward voyage. But they were becalmed for many days on their voyage to Havana, arriving much later than planned. It was late August, and the hurricane season had already begun. The fleet made hasty preparations for their return voyage and were ready to leave on September 4, 1622.

The 600-ton *Atocha* was one of the most important galleons in the

flotilla. She was a new ship, built in Havana and fitted with twenty bronze cannons. The *Atocha* was loaded with treasure to carry back to Spain. Her role was to sail in the rear of the convoy to protect the slower merchant ships. She took her position with the rest of the fleet that September morning and headed out across the Gulf of Mexico. The weather was fair and was expected to remain so.

The hurricane struck early the following day, September 5. Gale force winds tore at the ships, the waves towered threatening and black before tumbling onto the decks with a splintering crash. Sailors struggled with the rigging in a desperate attempt to save their ships. From the mastheads, those in the rear of the convoy could no longer

These gold bars bear the King of Spain's tax stamp. The Roman numerals indicate the carat and each dot above the numeral indicates the quarter carat.

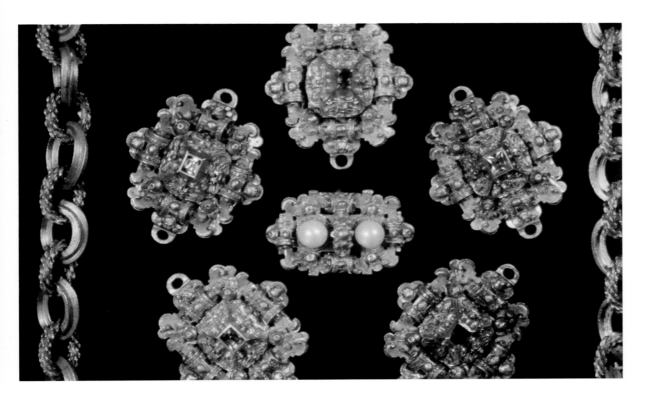

Pieces of Cinta belt inset with precious stones. This kind of jewelry was worn by both men and women in seventeenth century Spain.

see the leaders. The same terrified sailors could only watch as several of the smaller vessels sank helplessly beneath the waves.

The storm raged all through the day and on through the night. On the heaving decks of the *Atocha* and the *Santa Margarita*, the exhausted crew and passengers knelt and prayed. The ships were tossed around aimlessly, drifting with the ocean currents. Suddenly, there was blind panic as the two galleons were hurled toward the reefs and mangroves of the Florida Keys. There was no escape. Only about seventy passengers and crew from the two galleons survived when the ships ran aground on the reef and sank within sight of each other.

In all, eight ships were lost. In despair the captain of the fleet returned to Havana with the remaining twenty ships. He could not return to Spain without the gold the King expected. In Havana, he organized a salvage operation to raise the treasure from the *Atocha* and the *Santa Margarita.*

The salvagers had no idea where the *Santa Margarita* lay, but they quickly found the *Atocha.* She was lying with her mast still above the waterline in fifty-five feet of water. But her hatches were locked, and even the pearl divers who were later called upon to help could not get inside in water that deep. Then another hurricane struck. The tell-tale mast disappeared, the *Atocha's* hull broke up, and her whereabouts became a secret to be kept for over three centuries.

The Salvage Teams

Spain was desperately short of cash. The wars in Europe had almost emptied the Crown's coffers. The gold and silver carried aboard the *Atocha* and the *Santa Margarita* was urgently needed. Another salvage operation was mounted under the command of Francisco Nuñez Melián, who would receive a one-third share of the treasure from King Philip IV of Spain. A resourceful man, Melián invented a diving bell, cast in bronze, which was towed over the seabed, much like Mel Fisher's magnetometer. Inside the bell sat a slave, whose job it was to keep a look-out for the wrecks. In this way Melián found the *Santa Margarita* and salvaged some of the silver. But the *Atocha* was never found.

Today we have much more sophisticated equipment than Melián's diving bell. Without the help of modern technology, it is doubtful whether Mel Fisher would have been able to locate any of the *Atocha* treasure.

One of Fisher's partners, Fay Feild, developed the improved magnetometer that pinpointed the galleon anchor. Magnetometers are like powerful metal detectors. They consist of a sensor, which is attached underneath the boat and pulled through the water, connected to a display unit on the boat. If the sensor detects metal in the seabed below, a reading will be given on the unit. A buoy is thrown overboard at every reading, and divers examine the spot on the seabed. The only problem is that the buoys can be torn loose by bad weather or moved with the shifting sands below, leaving the true area unmarked.

The magnetometer sensor is towed up and down a course so that the whole of the seabed is covered. To keep the boat on course, the

Scientist Fay Feild checks out his invention, the magnetometer. It is towed behind a boat, close to the bottom and detects any ferrous metal on the seabed.

A theodolite operator prepares his tower for a long and hot day's work.

captain receives instructions by radio from two or more operators sitting in **theodolite towers**. Despite their hi-tech name, the towers themselves are just small, very uncomfortable, platforms built on stilts. There is no protection from the baking sun. It is hard for the operators to concentrate on their instruments so that they can guide the search boat through the sea and mark its course on their navigation charts. Inevitably, errors are made.

A more accurate alternative to the theodolites is the use of one of the electronic navigation systems now available. Fisher and his crew experimented with the Del Norte system, which uses radio signals to calculate the distance between its two towers and the boat. Position-fixing is said to be accurate to within three feet using this system. Fisher's crew were now aware of the slightest movement in their boats away from the exact spot where the magnetometer gave a reading.

Having located possible sites for the galleons using the magnetometer and position-fixing equipment, Fisher and his crew

One diver shows another a silver coin he has just uncovered using an airlift. Airlifts work like underwater vacuum cleaners.

Mailboxes like these deflect the wash from a boat's propellers downwards to uncover objects on the seabed.

next had to find out what had triggered the magnetometer. Often, the metal object would be lying under several feet of sand, far too heavy to remove by hand. For this job, Fisher used **mailboxes**, L-shaped tubes that fit over the boat's propellers. The mailboxes channel the wash from the propellers downward, blowing away the sand on the seabed to expose heavier objects beneath.

Mailboxes are obviously too powerful to use for any delicate work. Marine archaeologists working on the treasure sites need to record where artifacts were found, and one blast from the mailboxes could ruin hours of painstaking work.

A smaller hand-held device called an **airlift** is used to remove sand from around fragile objects. The airlift works on the same principle as a vacuum cleaner. It sucks in sand and stones, dumping them out through a tube. The heavier objects fall to the floor, and of course, any large objects would remain on the seabed, cleared of sand. Once, when using an airlift on the site of the *Atocha*, Fisher's divers were caught in a hail of uncut emeralds that the airlift threw out into the water.

The *Atocha* Cannons

Since the first finds in 1971, Mel Fisher and his crews had been working in the part of the search site they called the Bank of Spain. This shallow, sandy area of the Quicksands, to the west of the Marquesas Keys, was yielding treasure almost daily. In July 1973, Mel Fisher began to find the proof he so badly wanted: tangible evidence that he had found the site of the 1622 wrecks.

Fisher's crews were hard at work. The work boat *Southwind* used its mailboxes to blast a crater in the sandy seabed. The divers swam down to see what had been uncovered. John Lewis caught a glint of gold, and carefully pulled out a beautiful little rosary fashioned of pink coral beads and gold chain. Meanwhile, Mel Fisher's son Kane had found something perhaps less attractive, but far more important to the overall search for the lost galleons.

Kane didn't appreciate its value immediately: it looked like a loaf of bread sitting on the sea floor. But it was heavy, even underwater. Kane fought his way to the surface with his booty, suddenly realizing what he had found. It was a silver **ingot**, blackened by the seawater, weighing over 60 pounds. On the boat, it was seen to be stamped with the number 4584, its weight, and the level of purity of the silver. Could it be matched to one of the manifests? In high spirits, the other divers dived down into the sparkling sea. Two more numbered ingots were raised, and the excitement ran high.

The crew lost no time in racing back to Key West Harbor. They radioed ahead to ask Dr. Lyon to try to match the ingots against the manifests. On their arrival at the harbor, a huge crowd had gathered. The silver bars seemed to match some listed on the *Atocha's* manifest, and weighing scales had been pre-set on the quay to see whether the

A navigational device called an astrolabe is found to be in working order even after its long submersion in seawater.

A silver bar showing its identifying marks that were listed on the ship's manifest.

One of the Atocha's nine bronze cannons.

weight of the bar numbered 4584 would tally with the manifest. It did — precisely. Later, the second and third bars were also matched. Had Mel Fisher really found the *Atocha*, or was it, as some claimed, a coincidence? Could the bars have been transferred to another ship during the voyage? Could there have been other ships with similar ingots bearing the same numbers?

Fisher lived with this uncertainty for another two years. Not until 1975 was he able to prove without a shadow of a doubt that he had found the *Atocha*, or at least, parts of her.

It was going to be another scorching July day out on the water. The diving team had moved the search area to the southeast of the Bank of Spain at the suggestion of their new archaeologist, Duncan Matthewson III. The water was deeper, the seabed harder. Suddenly a scream shattered the quiet of the early Sunday morning. Angel Fisher rushed to the side of the boat, looking anxiously for her husband, Dirk, Mel Fisher's eldest son. Was it a shark attack? Dirk certainly looked like he was in trouble: he was shouting and yelling and waving his arms. Then Angel and the other crew members distinguished the word "cannon" in Dirk's frenzied shouts. Dirk had spotted five cannons, just lying there on the seabed!

Everyone hurriedly pulled on their scuba gear and swam down to take a look. Thirty feet away, Pat Clyne spied another four cannons, part-buried in sand. They all looked as though they had just tumbled off the deck of a rolling ship, with some piled one on top of the other. The position of each cannon was carefully mapped, while they were given an underwater inspection. The cannons Dirk had found had been badly worn, and no marks remained to identify them. But those cannons that had been protected under the sand bore the same marks as those on the *Atocha's* gun list. Here was indisputable proof. Mel Fisher had found the *Atocha*.

Raising a bronze cannon from its resting place of over 350 years.

The *Santa Margarita*

Treasure hunting is along, laborious job. Days and weeks can pass without finding much at all. Mel Fisher still left the dock each morning with a cheery "today's the day," but the crew's morale was often at a low ebb. Although he had found part of the *Atocha*, he had not found the hull where all the real treasure lay. Fisher knew from the *Atocha's* manifest that he would find a mass of gold and silver bars and coins in the main part of the ship. Where was it?

Fisher's crews were still finding coins in the Bank of Spain. Others searched the area where the cannons were found for clues as to where the *Atocha's* hull lay. Duncan Matthewson III was convinced that it lay in deep water, farther out in Hawk Channel. He had been studying the position of the cannons and other finds to try to work out the *Atocha's* route onto the reef. Somewhere along that route lay the hull — and the treasure.

The elusive treasure had still not been found by the end of 1979. In early 1980 Mel Fisher called a meeting with his crew. He felt they should consider concentrating their search on the *Santa Margarita* rather than the *Atocha*. They knew from the information in the Spanish archives that the *Santa Margarita* had sunk within sight of the *Atocha*. Now they knew the general area of the *Atocha's* sinking, perhaps the *Santa Margarita* would be easier to find. However, because the *Santa Margarita* already been part-salvaged by Melìan back in the seventeenth century, there would be less treasure.

Fisher hired an extra team under the leadership of Robert Jordan. The team was to search the area to the east of the cannons, and within two months they had found a small anchor and a number of silver coins. They could not be sure, though, whether these were part of the *Atocha* treasure or whether they were from the *Santa Margarita*.

The trail of artifacts led northward; the teams followed. The rewards were staggering. Among the pottery, silver coins, and weaponry they found gold bars, one of which weighed five pounds. It was obviously a large vessel — they were closing in on one of the galleons. It seemed logical for it to be the *Santa Margarita*, as the finds were being made some three miles to the east of the *Atocha* site. According to old eyewitness accounts, that was the distance between the two galleons when they went down.

In June 1980, Kane Fisher was swimming around the search site when he spotted something on the seabed. He dived down for a closer look. Six silver ingots, piles of ballast and several stacks of coins all molded together were sitting on the sea floor. Underneath all this treasure were the quiet wooden timbers of a large ship. Kane's heart leapt. He had found one of the galleons.

The whole team homed in on the find and busily set to work

A diver uses a small, hand-held airlift to carefully uncover objects buried in the sand.

mapping the area and photographing the hull of the galleon. For easy reference, a large plastic grid was laid over the whole of the hull. Whenever something was found, its precise location could be recorded on a chart giving a grid reference number.

Dr. Lyon now became a busy man, matching all the artifacts to the manifests. It was soon clear that this was the hull of the *Santa Margarita.*

The treasure was incredible! For the next eighteen months it seemed the flow was endless. Teams of divers brought up gold bars, silver ingots, and nearly 200 feet of gold chains. But the mysterious *Atocha* was still to be found.

Silver ingots on the deck of one of the salvage boats. Unlike gold, silver becomes blackened by the sea water.

One meter-square grids like these are used to measure and position artifacts that are found outside the main grid area of the site.

A display of some of the treasure from the Spanish galleons. Hundreds of feet of gold chain were found at the Santa Margarita site.

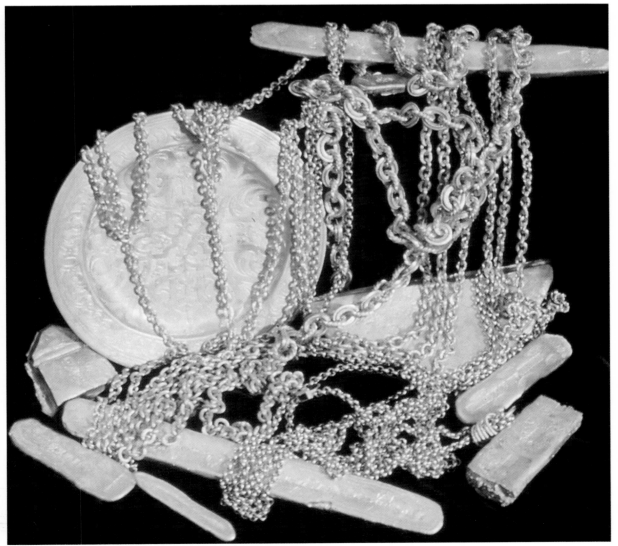

The *Atocha* is Found

The discovery of the *Santa Margarita* sparked a new enthusiasm in the crews. In 1982 the search for the *Atocha* took on a fresh start. It was difficult to know where to look. Some thought the hull would be found in the Quicksands, while others felt sure it was in the deeper water of Hawk Channel. It was a confusing time. Objects belonging to the *Atocha* were found in both places. In 1984, two galleon anchors and another cannon were brought up from the Quicksands, together with some smaller artifacts. Then, in 1985, the search turned toward Hawk Channel, where new clues were being found.

Duncan Matthewson III, the team archaeologist, had long ago briefed the divers to look out for large, heavy stones that would have been used as ballast in the galleons. These would have been laid in the ship's hull to weigh her down and give better stability. He surmised

Some of the thousands of emeralds found are displayed on gold chain.

27

Divers meticulously record and photograph the timbers of the Atocha's hull.

that when the galleon broke up, the ballast stones would have spilled out onto the ocean floor, leaving a trail the treasure hunters could follow. The stones would be many and large, and they should be easy to spot. Now the divers had picked up a trail of ballast stones out in Hawk Channel, which was leading them out southeastwards across the Channel. Maybe the *Atocha* was out there after all, as Duncan Matthewson had solidly maintained.

Eagerly, the team followed the trail. Confidence was restored, and the divers were in expectant moods. But as usual, it didn't happen overnight. Toward the end of May, their hard work was finally rewarded, first with a pile of gold bars, silver coins, jewelry, and silverware. Then they found uncut emeralds, weaponry, more ingots, and coins — thousands of silver coins. They were certain they had at last reached what they called the "motherlode" — the richest vein of gold. If they could find the chests of silver coins and all the silver ingots listed on the *Atocha's* manifest, they could at last be sure they had found the hull, and four hundred million dollars' worth of treasure.

On July 20, 1985 the ingots were located and with them, the *Atocha*. But she wasn't yet ready to give up her treasure. Before the divers could get down to begin mapping, a hurricane struck the area. All the boats were forced to return to Key West except one, which stayed behind to guard the site against intruders. The finding of the

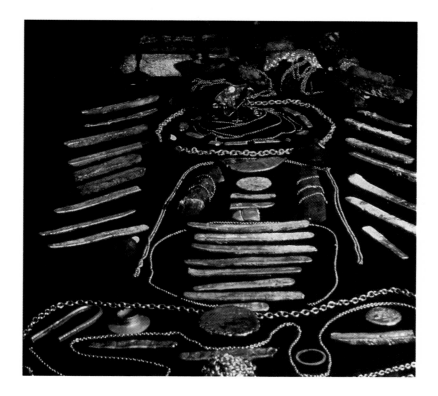

Atocha had been widely publicized, and it was possible that other people might try to get some of the gold for themselves. Work could not begin until the hurricane subsided. It was a long couple of days for the excited divers, who couldn't wait to dive down to see the wreck and her treasure.

Eventually, the hurricane subsided and the seas once again became clear as the sand settled. The work teams began. As with the salvage of the *Santa Margarita*, a large plastic grid was laid across the aged timbers of the galleon. All the artifacts were meticulously recorded on charts as they were carefully lifted from the sand. It was a slow process, and at times frustrating. It was hard for the excited divers to remember to follow this exacting procedure when they found especially beautiful pieces of treasure. It was, though, a very necessary part of their work, and one that enables us to learn more about life during the seventeenth century, both in Spain and in Central and South America.

The *Atocha's* treasure is as fabulous as Mel Fisher and his crew expected. Silver coins were found in hundreds of thousands, along with gorgeous pieces of gold and silver jewelry, some encrusted with magnificent South American emeralds, pearls, and coral. The treasure was not easy to find, but for Mel Fisher and all those who worked with him on the long project, through good and bad times, it was a real adventure.

Glossary

Airlift

A small hand-held dredge that works like a vacuum cleaner, used to clear away sand on the seabed.

Ingot

A bar of precious metal, such as gold, silver, or copper.

Magnetometer

A device that is used to detect metal underground or underwater.

Mailboxes

L-shaped tubes that deflect the wash from a boat's propellers downward to clear an area on the seabed.

Manifests

Shipping lists that itemize transactions during a voyage.

Theodolite Towers

Small platforms built on sticks where people use theodolites, instruments for position-fixing and navigation.

Index